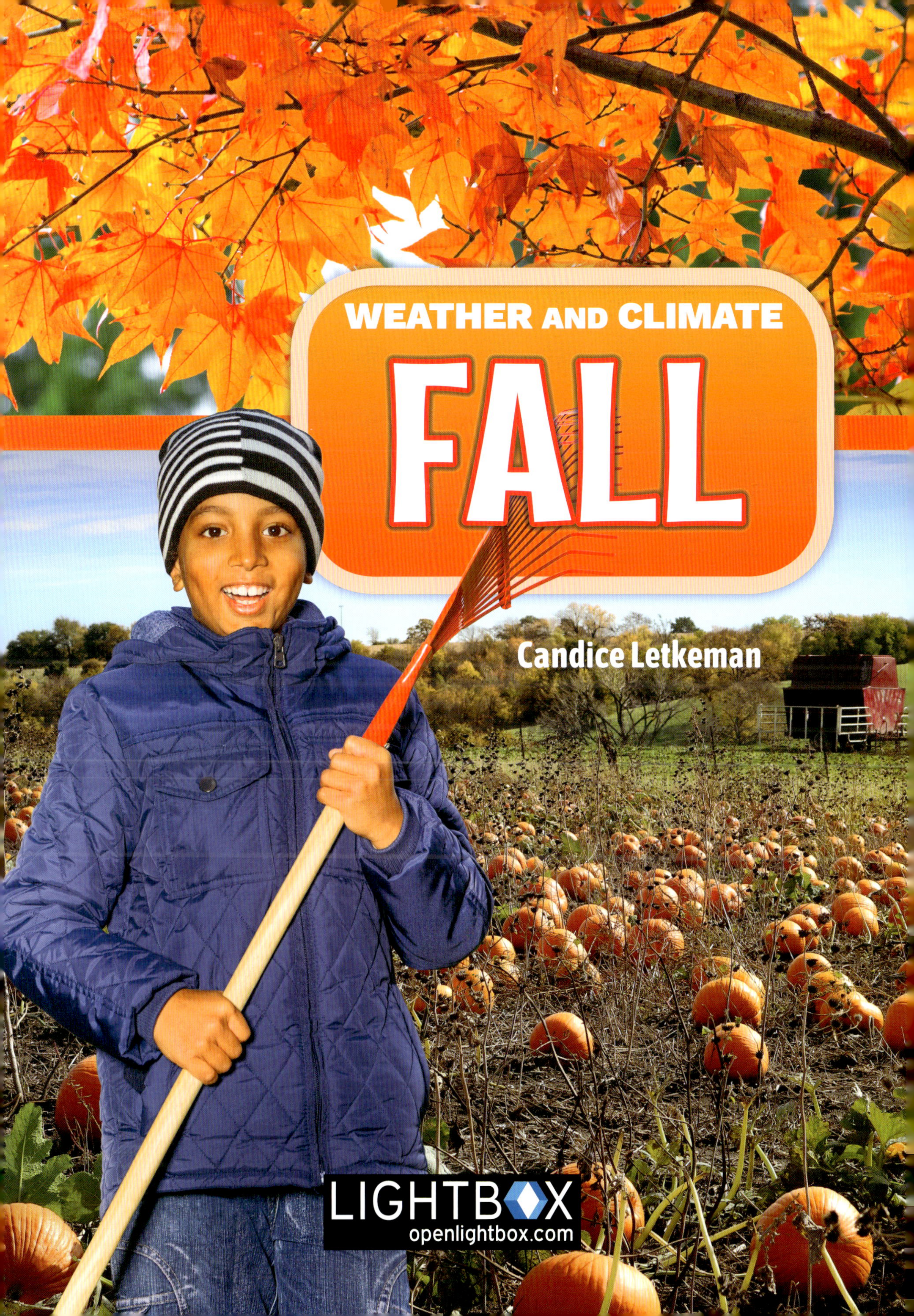
WEATHER AND CLIMATE
FALL
Candice Letkeman
LIGHTBOX
openlightbox.com

Go to
www.openlightbox.com
and enter this book's
unique code.

ACCESS CODE

LBXM9937

Lightbox is an all-inclusive digital solution for the teaching and learning of curriculum topics in an original, groundbreaking way. Lightbox is based on National Curriculum Standards.

STANDARD FEATURES OF LIGHTBOX

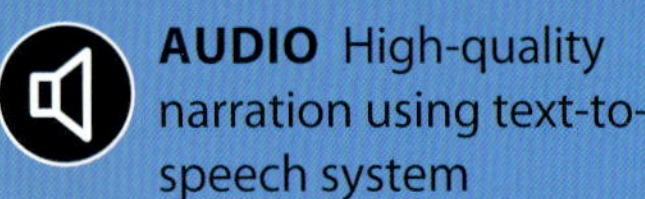
AUDIO High-quality narration using text-to-speech system

ACTIVITIES Printable PDFs that can be emailed and graded

SLIDESHOWS Pictorial overviews of key concepts

VIDEOS Embedded high-definition video clips

WEBLINKS Curated links to external, child-safe resources

TRANSPARENCIES Step-by-step layering of maps, diagrams, charts, and timelines

INTERACTIVE MAPS Interactive maps and aerial satellite imagery

QUIZZES Ten multiple choice questions that are automatically graded and emailed for teacher assessment

KEY WORDS Matching key concepts to their definitions

Copyright © 2020 Smartbook Media Inc. All rights reserved.

Contents

Fantastic Fall

The **world's largest pumpkin** was grown in Belgium in 2016. It weighed **2,624 pounds** (1,190 kilograms).

Each fall, **millions of monarch butterflies** fly to Mexico from Canada and the United States. Many travel more than **3,000 miles** (4,828 kilometers).

Fall is the season between summer and winter. It is also known as autumn. The weather becomes cooler during this season. Leaves start to fall.

Squirrels gather food in fall for the coming winter. They bury nuts and seeds. Deer grow thicker fur in fall. This helps them stay warm. Birds such as Canada geese usually **migrate** in fall. They need to go where it is warm.

What does fall mean for you? Is it a time to collect colorful leaves? Do you and your friends play football? Maybe you and your family carve pumpkins. Fall is the best time for these activities. Imagine how your perfect fall would look.

Fall in the United States

Fall is usually from September to November. The weather varies across the country. Northern states are often cooler than southern states. Leaves start to change color earlier in northern regions.

HAWAI'I

Hawai'i has the heaviest fall rains in the United States. Mount Waialeale, Hawai'i, is one of the wettest places in the world.

Can You Find Your State?

Find your state on the map. What color is it? Find the same color in the legend.

What is the average temperature of your state in fall?

Legend
Degrees Fahrenheit (°F)

- 25–35
- 35–45
- 45–50
- 50–55
- 55–60
- 60–65
- 65–70
- 70–75
- Other countries
- Water

Scale 0 250 miles / 250 km

The Weather in Fall

It takes one year for Earth to travel around the Sun. The seasons change four times. Around June, the northern half of Earth leans toward the Sun and is warmed. This half experiences summer. At the same time, the southern half leans away. It becomes cooler and experiences winter.

In spring and fall, both **hemispheres** receive a similar amount of warmth from the Sun. Earth is not tilted toward the Sun or away from it. Fall begins in the Northern Hemisphere in September. The fall **equinox** falls on September 23.

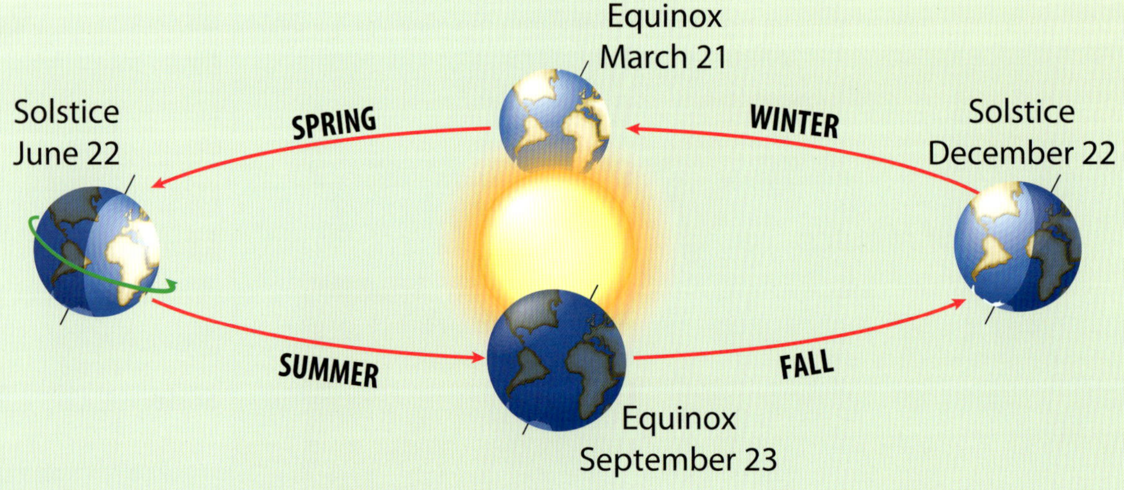

An Average Fall Season

From September to November, there are about 700 hours of sunshine in San Diego, California.

Approximately how many hours of sunshine does Tampa get in a fall season? What about Syracuse and Dallas?

Which of these four states has the most rain and snow in fall? Which has the least?

= 100 hours

= 1 inch (2.5 centimeters)

People who live on the coast are most at risk from hurricanes.

Extreme Fall

Extreme weather in fall causes accidents and destroys property. **Natural disasters** such as hurricanes lead to a great deal of damage.

HURRICANES

Tropical cyclones are circular storms that form over warm oceans. The tropical cyclones that form over the Atlantic Ocean or eastern Pacific Ocean are called hurricanes. Hurricanes bring heavy rains and strong winds. They sometimes cause **floods**. Hurricanes can destroy buildings and rip out trees from their roots.

FOG

Fog is like a cloud near to the ground. The longer, cooler nights in fall can cause fog. It can be difficult to see in fog. Drivers may have accidents. Sometimes, airplanes cannot take off.

SNOWSTORMS

Snow can be heavy and wet in fall. Tree branches can break, damaging houses and power lines. Roads can become icy and dangerous for driving.

Extreme Fall Timeline

Many places in the United States experience fog in fall. Hurricanes often make **landfall** at this time of year.

August–September 1994
Hurricane John forms over the eastern Pacific Ocean. It lasts 31 days, becoming the longest-lasting hurricane ever recorded.

October 2005
Hurricane Wilma makes landfall in Florida. It is the strongest hurricane ever recorded over the Atlantic Ocean.

November 2007
Dense fog in Fresno, California, causes a large highway accident. More than 100 vehicles are involved.

October 2012
Hurricane Sandy hits New Jersey. Over the next few days, 24 states are affected by the storm. Repairing the damage costs about $71 billion.

November 2012
Fog causes more than 100 flights to be canceled at Chicago's O'Hare airport.

October 2018
Hurricane Michael causes power outages across four states. More than 1 million people are left without power.

Weather Tools over Time

People have been studying weather for thousands of years. They have found patterns in the way the weather changes each year. These patterns help them **predict** what type of weather will come in the future. Over time, many tools have been developed to help predict and record the weather.

THERMISTOR

Thermistors measure the temperature of the ocean. They stay in one place in the ocean. They can stay in the water for a long time.

Michael Faraday invented the thermistor in 1833. He was a physicist and chemist.

ANEMOMETER

Anemometers measure wind speed. Some also measure the direction of the wind. Wind direction is described by noting where the wind is coming from. A west wind means the wind is blowing from the west and going toward the east.

The anemometer was invented by Leon Battista Alberti around 1450. Anemometers are important tools for meteorologists.

OCEANOGRAPHIC SATELLITE

Satellites travel around Earth. They can collect and send data from devices in the sea. This data is quickly sent to computers on land. It helps oceanographers study weather patterns at sea.

The National Aeronautics and Space Administration (NASA) launched Seasat on June 26, 1978. It was the first satellite to help study the ocean.

Discover Scientists

Scientists want to understand the world around us. They try to find out why things happen. You can be a scientist, too. Learn about what different kinds of scientists do.

Chemists study substances and the changes that happen when substances combine.

Meteorologists study and predict the weather.

Physical oceanographers study ocean temperatures, levels, and **currents**.

Fall Technology Today

Technology can protect people from dangerous weather. Some inventions help people stay aware. Other discoveries protect the environment.

FOG LIGHTS

Fog lights are special lights on the front of cars. When turned on, they shine low to the ground. This angle helps drivers see road edges and highway lines. Drivers must always drive slowly when fog lights are needed.

Some cars have rear fog lights. They can be seen by drivers in the cars behind.

ROAD DE-ICING SOLUTIONS

Rock salt is often used to de-ice, or remove ice, from roads. However, it can pollute land, rivers, and lakes. Cheese brine or beet molasses can be used instead of rock salt. They are safe for the environment. Cheese brine is water full of a different salt. It melts the ice on roads quickly. Beet molasses is made from sugar beets. Some states use beet molasses to de-ice roads.

Winter service vehicles are often used to spread de-icing solutions on roads.

SOCIAL MEDIA AND MESSAGING APPS

Some apps allow people to send messages for help during a hurricane. People can share information, even when there is no power. Friends and neighbors can quickly help each other. People can also use apps to let their friends and family know they are safe.

Residents were rescued from flooded nursing homes in Texas during Hurricane Harvey. A tweet for help was retweeted about 4,500 times.

Hurricane Shelters

Most U.S. hurricanes make landfall on the country's Gulf and Atlantic coasts. These areas may have hurricane shelters. People can go to hurricane shelters to stay safe during a hurricane.

Shape

Structures with multiple sides have more surfaces for the wind to blow against. The wind cannot build up enough pressure on any one side to cause damage. Instead, it flows around the building.

Pier Foundation

Piers raise a building up from the ground. They are dug deep into the ground to support the structure. Floodwater from a hurricane goes under the building. The building stays dry.

Hurricane shutters
Strong winds can blow in windows and cause damage inside the building. Hurricane shutters protect windows from flying debris. Hurricane shutters are made from metal, plastics, or plywood.
Steel Roof
A steel roof will not rip apart in high winds. It keeps the building dry. Four or more sloping sides of a roof stand up to strong winds better than two sides.
In 1961, Hurricane Esther became the first hurricane to be photographed from space.
September is the most common month for hurricanes in the United States.

Hurricane Safety

Being outside in a hurricane is dangerous. During a hurricane, people may have to stay in their houses for a long time. The electricity can stop working. Water from the faucet might not be safe to drink. Some families have plans so they are ready for hurricanes. They know where safe places are and how to get there.

An emergency kit holds supplies for when they are needed. The kit should always be ready.

A radio helps keep people informed. Radios report on the weather and when it is safe to go outside.

There should be enough canned food and bottled water for at least three days.

A flashlight and batteries should be in the kit in case the power goes out.

Find Signs of Fall

What signs of fall do you see where you live?

1. Make a list of things you see in fall. Use these pictures as examples to help you.
2. Go for a walk around your yard, schoolyard, or neighborhood. Look for signs of fall.
3. Check items off your list as you see them.

Fall around the World

POLAR CLIMATE ZONE

The polar zone is the coldest climate zone. Open water freezes up in fall. Temperatures drop and daylight hours decrease. By mid-fall, there is no sunlight during the day in regions near the North and South Poles.

Wildlife: Arctic Fox, Arctic Wolf, Penguin, Polar Bear

TEMPERATE CLIMATE ZONE

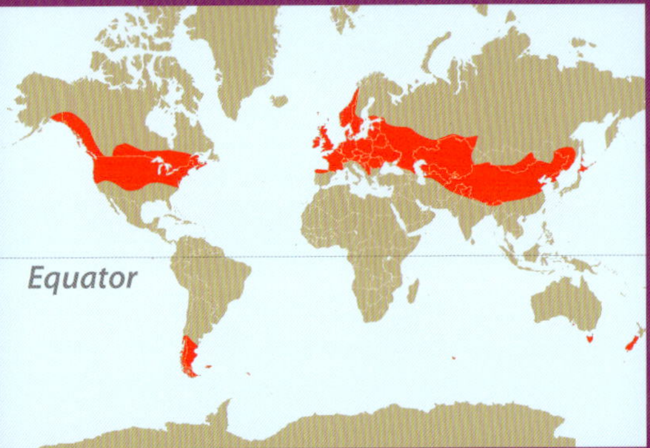

The temperate zone has four very different seasons. These are winter, spring, summer, and fall. Most temperate land is north of the equator. Temperatures become cooler in fall. Many trees lose their leaves.

Wildlife: Giant Panda, Raccoon, Red Fox, Squirrel

Fall is different around the world. An imaginary line called the equator circles Earth, dividing it into two halves. Places close to the equator are often hot all year. Areas far from the equator are cold. Earth has four major **climate** zones.

SUBTROPICAL CLIMATE ZONE

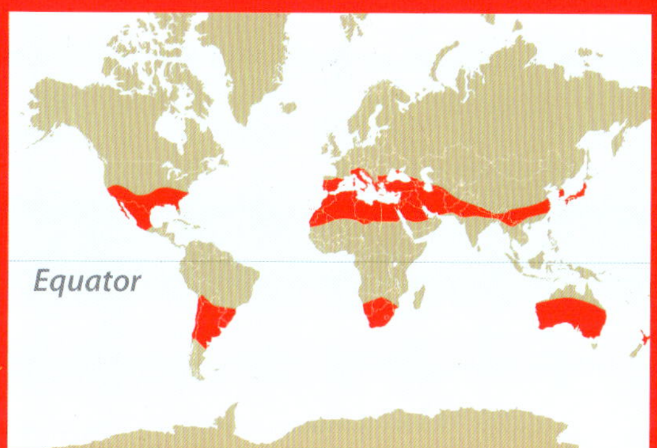

The subtropical zone has a warm or hot climate. Summer and winter are the two main seasons. Fall is a short transitional season. Tropical zones may be dry or humid. In humid subtropical areas, rain falls evenly throughout the year.

Wildlife: Alligator, Kangaroo, Leopard, Python

TROPICAL CLIMATE ZONE

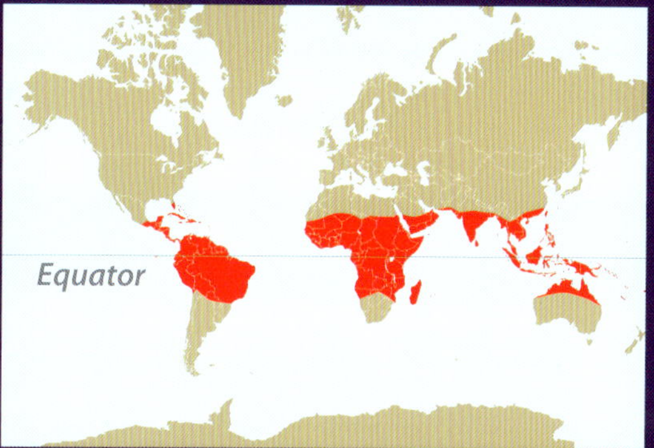

The tropical zone is the hottest climate zone. It does not have a fall season. The weather is hot all year. Some places in this zone are humid. There are areas that receive 10 inches (254 millimeters) or more of rain in a month.

Wildlife: Gorilla, Komodo Dragon, Orangutan, Rhinoceros

Quiz

1 What type of scientist studies and predicts weather?

A: Meteorologist

2 What is another name for fall?

A: Autumn

3 Which state has the most hurricanes?

A: Florida

4 What type of weather is like a cloud low to the ground?

A: Fog

5 What materials are used to make hurricane shutters?

A: Metal, plastics, or plywood

6 How long does it take for Earth to travel around the Sun?

A: One year

7 What are two de-icing solutions that are safe for the environment?

A: Beet molasses and cheese brine

8 How much food should be in an emergency kit?

A: Enough for at least three days

9 Which climate zone has no sunlight by mid-fall?

A: Polar climate zone

10 How far do monarch butterflies travel in fall?

A: More than 3,000 miles (4,828 km)

Key Words

climate: the average weather of an area over a period of time

currents: bodies of water or air moving in a specific direction

debris: the scraps of something broken down or destroyed

equinox: when the Sun is directly over the equator and a day has equal hours of sunlight and darkness

floods: great flows of water that rise up and spread over the land

fog: tiny drops of water floating in the air near the ground

hemispheres: the two halves of Earth, especially above and below the equator

hurricane: a circular storm that forms over warm oceans, bringing high winds, heavy rains, and sometimes floods

landfall: arriving on land after traveling by sea or air

migrate: to move from one place to another at different times of year

natural disasters: events caused by forces of nature that lead to destruction of life and property

predict: to say that something will happen in the future

satellites: human-made objects that are sent into space and orbit, or travel around, Earth

Index

LIGHTBOX

SUPPLEMENTARY RESOURCES

Click on the plus icon found in the bottom left corner of each spread to open additional teacher resources.

- Download and print the book's quizzes and activities
- Access curriculum correlations
- Explore additional web applications that enhance the Lightbox experience

LIGHTBOX DIGITAL TITLES

Packed full of integrated media

VIDEOS

INTERACTIVE MAPS

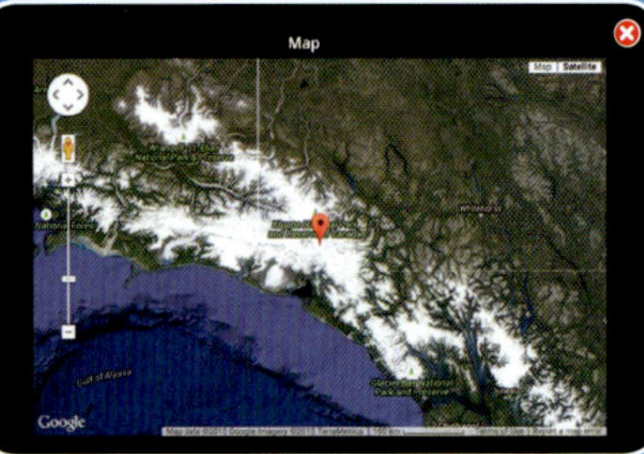

WEBLINKS

SLIDESHOWS

QUIZZES

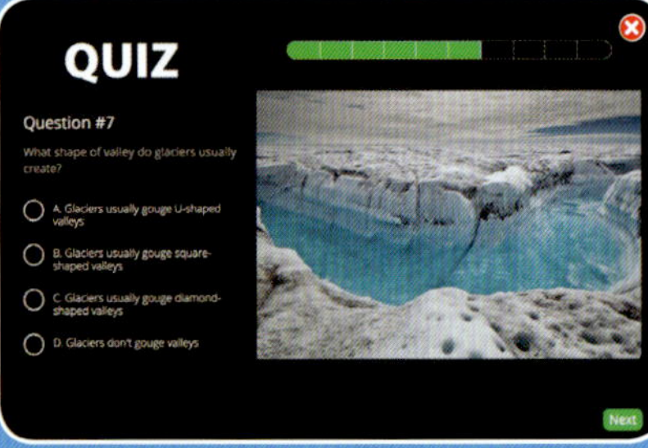

OPTIMIZED FOR

✓ TABLETS
✓ WHITEBOARDS
✓ COMPUTERS
✓ AND MUCH MORE!

Published by Smartbook Media Inc.
350 5th Avenue, 59th Floor New York, NY 10118
Website: www.openlightbox.com

Copyright © 2020 Smartbook Media Inc.
All rights reserved. No part of this publication may be reproduced, stored in a retrieval system, or transmitted in any form or by any means, electronic, mechanical, photocopying, recording, or otherwise, without the prior written permission of the publisher.

Library of Congress Control Number: 2019942192

ISBN 978-1-5105-4509-0 (hardcover)
ISBN 978-1-5105-4510-6 (multi-user eBook)

Printed in Guangzhou, China
1 2 3 4 5 6 7 8 9 0 23 22 21 20 19

062019
122718

Project Coordinator: Priyanka Das
Designer: Ana María Vidal

Photo Credits
Every reasonable effort has been made to trace ownership and to obtain permission to reprint copyright material. The publisher would be pleased to have any errors or omissions brought to its attention so that they may be corrected in subsequent printings. The publisher acknowledges Getty Images, iStock, Shutterstock, Alamy, and Dreamstime as its primary image suppliers for this title.